^{TM}

ADVENTURE GAME BOOKS

DINOBOT WAR

Earth has been invaded by the
powerful robots from the distant
planet Cybertron – the Heroic
Autobots and their enemies, the Evil
Decepticons. They can disguise their
robot shapes as earthly machines and
transform for battle at lightning
speed. The battle between Good and
Evil rages on Earth . . .

Also published by Young Corgi Books:

THE TRANSFORMERS™: PERIL FROM THE STARS
by Dave Morris

ADVENTURE GAME BOOKS

Dinobot War

Dave Morris
Illustrated by Bob Harvey

YOUNG CORGI BOOKS

THE TRANSFORMERS™: DINOBOT WAR

A YOUNG CORGI BOOK 0 552 523143

First publication in Great Britain.

PRINTING HISTORY

Young Corgi edition published 1985
Young Corgi edition reprinted 1986 (twice)

Young Corgi Books are published by Transworld
Publishers Ltd., 61–63 Uxbridge Road, Ealing,
London W5 5SA.

Made and printed in Great Britain by the
Guernsey Press Co. Ltd., Guernsey, Channel Islands.

This is an adventure story. But it is not like most other adventure stories — there is one big difference.

You are the main character.

What happens in the story depends on **your** decisions. The fate of the Transformers — whether the valiant Dinobots will prevail or whether the evil schemes of the Decepticons will succeed — is in **your** hands.

Do not read the pages of this adventure in numerical order, as you would an ordinary book. You should start at page **1**, of course, but where you go to from there will depend on what you choose to do.

Prepare yourself to meet The Transformers!

NOW TURN TO PAGE 1 . . .

You are on your first visit to Disneyland in California. In a single morning you have sailed safely past a pirate battle on the Spanish Main, crept nervously through a ghost-infested mansion, taken a trip on an old paddle-steamer and plunged on a breakneck ride through a mountain. Now you are riding on a train that twists and winds its way through Disneyland. You find yourself passing scenes of prehistoric times where animated models of giant reptiles clash gorily.

As you get down from the train you decide to look for a hot dog stand. Then you notice some kind of disturbance up ahead. Security guards and police are moving people away from a barrier. Beyond the barrier, you can see signs advertising a new attraction now under construction. You wonder why the crowds are being moved away, and you decide to investigate.

If you try to sneak past the barrier, turn to page 3
If you climb into the electrically-powered buggy nearby and try to drive past the guards, turn to page 2

You clamber into the buggy. It is a simple vehicle, which goes at walking speed, used by Disney staff to cruise the streets. A Walkman rests on the seat next to you. You glance at the cassette in it: *Cats*, the soundtrack from the musical. Looking across the controls of the buggy, you find them simple enough. You press a button and the motor purrs quietly.

If you wish to leave the Walkman here, turn to page **3**
If you keep the Walkman with you as you drive past the barrier, turn to page **4**

'Hey, kid!'

You jump as the guard's loud voice blares in your ear. You try to a dash for it, but he grabs your arm. 'This area's off limits,' he tells you. 'You can't go past this point.'

You are determined to get a sneak preview of the new attraction — and to find out what's so mysterious that they have to put a up barrier. What will you tell the guard:

That you are a messenger with important papers to deliver? Turn to page 11

That your father is a Disney executive and is supervising the new attraction? Turn to page 12

The little buggy trundles slowly towards the guards. As you approach them, your nerve begins to fail. You are sure they will stop you. But then you are on the far side of the barrier and driving towards the new attraction. Amazingly, it is as though the guards didn't even see you!

The new exhibit, The Wizard's Cave, is at the end of the street. No-one is about, though you can see power cables running into the cave mouth and it is obvious that people are working inside. You stop the buggy outside Droid Hunter, an attraction that is closed for repair.

If you enter the Droid Hunter attraction, turn to page **5**
If you go on and enter the Wizard's Cave, turn to page **10**

Although the attraction is not open, the gates are unlocked and you have no trouble getting inside. Droid Hunter consists of a network of ramps and gantries where you can hunt automated targets using harmless laser rifles. It is deathly quiet. Your footsteps echo eerily as you tread along a futuristic walkway. Lights come on automatically as you pass, but they do not give much light. You take a laser rifle down from the rack on the wall. You switch on the Walkman you found in the buggy, thinking that some music will make the deserted place seem less creepy, but nothing happens. You are surprised to find that the cassette is gone.

If you wish to stay here, turn to page **6**
If you decide to go back outside, turn to page **3**

An alarming impression creeps into your mind. You think something is following you, stalking through the shadows noiselessly. Trying to convince yourself that it is just a trick of your imagination, you look back over your shoulder. In the deep darkness behind, you glimpse two tiny pinpricks of green light. Like eyes. Your heart leaps.

Will you run? If so, turn to page **7**
If you stand your ground, turn to page **8**

With a yell you drop your laser-rifle and race along the shadowy ramp. Something is definitely pursuing you – you hear its stealthy footfalls hard on your heels, and somehow you know that it is not human!

Suddenly you crash into something solid. You have run straight into a dark mirror. You stare at your own reflection. Behind you, you see a catlike being getting ready to spring. You can do nothing to save yourself, and this is

THE END

You stand your ground and stare into the shadows. 'Okay!' you hear yourself saying. 'Whoever's there, come on and show yourself.'

You are answered by a terrible sound that makes you quake with terror. At first you mistake it for the screech of feedback on a hi-fi, but then you realize that it was actually the growl of a hunting cat. A dark shape bounds along the ramp towards you, and you catch a glimpse of metallic fangs . . .

You are almost paralyzed with fright, but you manage to raise the laser-rifle. Your attacker is directly in front of you as you pull the trigger. Normally the laser-beams of these rifles are quite harmless, but at such close range they can be dazzling. The creature must be sensitive to bright light − you hear it whine in pain and rage and then scurry off.

You throw down the laser-rifle and run out into the sunshine.

Turn to page 10

9

You decide to take a look at the Wizard's Cave instead. You enter a tunnel strung with spotlights. Sturdy wooden posts hold up the roof and walls. The Wizard's Cave is due to open in only a few weeks, and yet there is no sign of the bustling activity you would expect. Why has work stopped? You hear voices ahead, and tiptoe towards them.

Turn to page **13**

Your story does not convince the guard. 'Well, if you have any important papers,' he says, 'I'll take 'em inside.'

He holds out a beefy hand and waits, grinning because he knows you are not a messenger.

You go away and console yourself with a burger and a milk shake.

You spend the afternoon enjoying the other sights of Disneyland – but you very nearly had a true-life adventure that would have been far more incredible. You can only find out about *that* by turning back to page 1, because this is

THE END

He looks doubtful, but finally he says, 'Can't do any harm to check.' He takes a radio from his belt. Your heart sinks. It will not take him long to find out that you are lying and you will probably be thrown out of Disneyland.

Just as he is speaking into the radio, however, an elderly woman comes striding over the barrier. 'What is this, young man?' she demands as she waves her umbrella in the guard's face. 'You're a bit big to be picking on children, aren't you?'

While the confused guard tries to explain to her, you slip away and head towards the new attraction – The Wizard's Cave.

Turn to page 10

Reaching the end of the tunnel, you look out across a floodlit chamber. A few workmen and security guards are standing by while five men in suits talk intently. Your gaze travels around the chamber. You see plans and chalked guidelines for the layout of the Wizard's Cave, but it seems that work has stopped.

The five suited men are obviously in charge here. One of them, a thin man wearing thick spectacles, is holding a curious device that looks like a very heavy rifle. He is talking to the others about it, and if you strain your ears you can just about catch what they're saying.

If you wish to listen to what they are saying, turn to page **14**

If you try creeping past them to investigate the rest of the chamber, turn to page **16**

They are discussing the strange rifle, and you hear one of them refer to it as a 'Stasis Gun'. They are obviously very excited by what they have discovered about its powers. It seems that the Stasis Gun has the power to 'freeze' objects in time. You watch in fascination as the scientist throws a coin into the air. A blast from the Stasis Gun freezes it, causing it to hang unsupported in midair until he unfreezes it with a second blast and allows it to continue falling!

'Let's fetch some torches,' you hear him say to the other men, 'and I'll show you what else we found.'

They are coming over towards you. To avoid detection, you have to slip along the wall of the chamber.

Turn to page 16

You edge through the shadows by the wall of the chamber, hardly daring to breathe in case you are spotted and thrown out. Luckily, everyone's attention is on what the scientists are saying. In the gloom at the back of the chamber, you come across a strange object. It appears to be a flying saucer, partially buried in the rock wall. Could it really be from another planet — perhaps abandoned by alien visitors in Earth's distant past, an abandoned craft that has waited millions of years to be excavated?

You are amazed — even a little frightened — but you want to find out. You make your way towards the saucer.

Turn to page **17**

Your foot catches on a metal briefcase. It makes a scraping sound on the cavern floor, but the others do not notice. By touching a panel on the side of the case, you cause it to flip open. Inside is an assortment of strange items. You are quite sure that they were not made by any human hand.

Suddenly the beam of a torch plays upon you. You are dazzled by the light and hear a man cry out. Running footsteps move towards you.

Turn to page 18

The men close in around you, shining their torches at you. 'Hey, it's just a kid,' says one. 'That's a relief,' murmurs one of the workmen; 'I thought it was an alien come to life!'

A security guard strides over to you. 'Hey,' he says, 'you're not allowed in here – '

What can you do now? If you allow them to take you out of the cavern, you will never find out the truth behind the saucer. You could be missing the most amazing adventure of your life! But what else *can* you do?

If you give yourself up, this is THE END
If you try using one of the items in the case, turn to page
19

You reach into the case and you pull out large metal sphere with a dial on it. You don't know what it does, but there is only one way to find out . . .

Turning the dial may be very foolish, but with several guards about to seize you, you are not thinking too clearly. As you move the dial, you see them stare in shock and then begin to disappear in a whirling haze of light. The light soon grows so bright that you have to cover your eyes. Just before you do, you fancy that you see a giant cat leaping towards you.

You have no time now to think about it. You are passing out . . .

Turn to page 21

You slowly recover consciousness. You are lying on your back in the midst of a steaming jungle. Mist swirls thickly all around you, barely muffling the animal cries that echo distantly through the strange land.

Suddenly a deafening roar thunders out, chilling you to the marrow of your bones. You hear something moving towards you — something *large*. The creature appears as a monstrous, pale silhouette against the mist.

Will you run away? If so, turn to page **24**
If you hide and wait to see what is coming, turn to page **22**

A towering saurian shape lumbers into view. It is unmistakably a tyrannosaurus – but a mechanical one! It is much more sophisticated than the animated dinosaur models you saw in Disneyland. This one moves like a living creature. You feel a tingle of dread as it peers at the bush you are crouching behind.

'What have we here?' it says abruptly. 'A puny human.' You can hardly believe this – it *talks*! And it seems to have spotted you . . .

Terrified, you run blindly into the undergrowth. You seem to have reached safety when suddenly another voice comes from right behind you, making you jump in surprise. You turn around to find a robot bronto- saurus looking at you.

Turn to page 26

You run until you reach a river frothy with strange lichen. The monster may have heard you. It is stomping closer, smashing small trees aside like matchwood. You look around frantically. Nearby are some small bushes where you could hide. A number of muddy boulders form stepping-stones across the river, so you could try to get to the opposite bank.

If you try to hide, turn to page **22**
If you try to cross the river, turn to page **25**

You leap from boulder to boulder. They are slippery, but large enough so that you are in no danger of falling off into the swirling waters. Just as you reach the boulder in the middle of the river, however, it lurches sickeningly and you are thrown off balance. Clinging to the boulder for dear life, you are horrified to see that you are being raised up into the air. Now you realize that this is not a boulder at all — it feels like metal, and two gleaming eyes peer up at you. You are lifted up on the head of a mechanical brontosaurus!

He slowly heaves his bulk out of the muddy river and then dips his head down, enabling you to scramble onto the safety of firm ground.

Turn to page 26

The robot brontosaurus watches you with intelligent eyes and you relax a little. 'Aha, a human youngster,' it says.

You are not surprised that it can talk – after all, if you can accept the idea of a huge, intelligent robot dinosaur, why *shouldn't* it be able to talk?

'What are you doing here?' asks the robot.

If you say that you are running away from a monster,
turn to page **28**
If you say that you don't know, turn to page **29**

'Oh, dear!' says the brontosaurus, with more than a hint of alarm in his voice. 'I don't want to run into any monsters. We'd better get out of here.'

He leads you off through the dense foliage that fringes the swamps.

'This is my kind of territory,' announces the brontosaurus. 'My name is SLUDGE, and I am particularly skilled at jungle warfare.'

You introduce yourself and ask him where you are.

'Well, in fact I'm – *listen*, did you hear that?' A thunderous bellow rumbles through the mist. You see a blossom of purple light off to your left, quickly followed by the harsh sound of a laser hissing through the damp air. SLUDGE is uncertain as to what he should do.

If you think he should investigate what is happening, turn to page 36

If you suggest heading quickly away in the opposite direction, turn to page 42

The mighty robot dips his head down. 'I'm supposed to be meeting my fellow Dinobots near here,' he tells you.

Before you can answer, a gleaming saurian shape comes crashing through the undergrowth. Nervously, you edge around behind the brontosaurus — at least *he* seems friendly, but the newcomer is a robot tyrannosaurus and looks very fierce indeed!

Turn to page **30**

The two giant robots obviously recognize one another. It seems that the tyrannosaurus, whose name is GRIMLOCK, is in charge. He barely notices you and then stalks off into the swirling fog. 'SLUDGE,' he calls back to the other gruffly, 'follow me. Bring the human if you wish.'

SLUDGE starts to reply, but GRIMLOCK is too far off. 'We'd better hurry,' he says to you. 'He won't be pleased if I get myself lost . . .'

If you want to go with the Dinobots, turn to page 33
If you tell SLUDGE to go on without you, turn to page 31

'Well, I really think you ought to come with us, you know,' protests SLUDGE. 'This is no place to go wandering about on your own.'

*If you decide to accompany him, turn to page **33***
*If you insist on staying here, turn to page **32***

You watch them disappear into the mist. You are alone in the jungle. A strange bird, like no flying creature you have ever seen, screeches as it flutters from bush to bush. Dragonflies hover to and fro.

You begin to trudge through the trees. The ground is muddy and squelchy, which slows you down. Suddenly you notice that the birds have stopped singing. There is a disturbing silence . . .

Alarmed, you stare at the trees all around you. A throaty growl comes from nearby. You see a feline shape padding towards you. A great cat has chosen you as its prey.

What will you do now:

Approach the cat? Turn to page **46**
Climb a tree? Turn to page **47**
Run for your life? Turn to page **48**

With you straddling his armoured shoulders, SLUDGE lumbers off after his leader. GRIMLOCK takes little notice of either of you. He holds a small device in his hands and sweeps it around him as he walks.

'I'm picking up a reading,' says GRIMLOCK after a while.

There is a loud shriek from high above and a winged form descends from the overcast sky. At first you think that it is swooping to attack, and you cling desperately to SLUDGE's neck. Then you see the dull sheen of burnished metal – it is another robot, a pterodactyl this time.

Turn to page **34**

'SWOOP!' calls out GRIMLOCK to the newcomer as he glides towards you. 'Have you found the others yet?'

'Of course I have,' jeers SWOOP. 'I can see much further from up here than you can on the ground. SLAG is spoiling for a battle – as usual – but SNARL is weak, from the lack of sunlight.'

SWOOP wheels, and flaps away across the treetops. He makes no allowance for the fact that you cannot move so quickly on the ground, and GRIMLOCK and SLUDGE have to break into a lumbering run to keep up with him. He leads you to a clearing where two more robots await you.

'The Dinobots are assembled,' snarls GRIMLOCK. 'Let the Decepticons beware!'

Now turn to page **38**

34

SLUDGE carries you through the marshes. His large feet are well-suited to the ground, and it does not take long to reach the scene of the disturbance.

As the mists roll back, you see two robot warriors locked in combat. The larger is a mechanical tyrannosaurus. He seems more powerful than the sleek cat-like robot he is fighting, but the latter moves with such ferocity and grace that the tyrannosaurus's snapping jaws cannot strike home.

'That is GRIMLOCK, our leader,' murmurs SLUDGE, referring to the tyrannosaurus. 'He should be able to beat RAVAGE – '

But SLUDGE has spoken too soon. GRIMLOCK, stepping back to avoid RAVAGE's attack, fails to notice a mudpool just behind him. He plunges into the marsh, and as he struggles to wade free RAVAGE takes aim with his deadly proton missiles.

SLUDGE hesitates. He knows he must act to save GRIMLOCK, but he does not know what to do.

*If you suggest he charges RAVAGE, turn to page **43***
*If you think he should stamp the ground with his massive foot, turn to page **44***

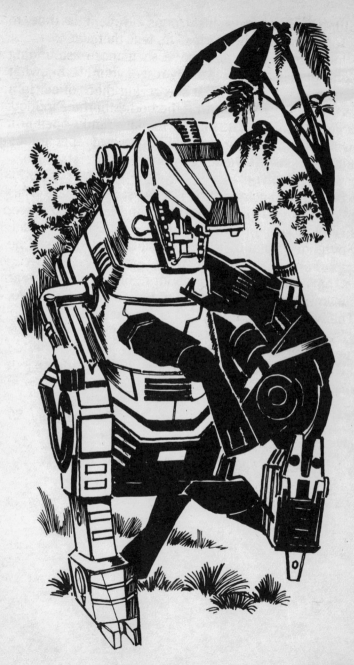

GRIMLOCK surveys his troops. 'Now it is time to resume our Autobot forms,' he tells them.

In the past hour you have seen more astounding sights than in the whole of the rest of your life, but what happens now is the most staggering thing of all. In a series of clicks and whirrs, the bodies of the Dinobots begin to change. The mighty metallic flanks open and swing back, rearranging their outward appearance until five sword-wielding robot warriors stand in a circle around you.

SNARL's transformation is slowest. As the last of his golden armour pieces swing up and latch into place, this mighty robot sways. 'My solar cells are not receiving enough sunlight in this mist-shrouded place,' he says. 'I am sluggish.'

'That's the worst thing about California in the year four million BC,' says SWOOP to you with a chuckle. 'The weather's so lousy!'

You almost pass out from shock. Your worst fear has been confirmed − the strange device you found beside the saucer has somehow carried you back millions of years in time!

Turn to page 39

'Doubtless you are all wondering why I have summoned you here,' says GRIMLOCK to the other Dinobots. The Dinobots grumble, especially SLAG and SWOOP. 'Silence!' roars GRIMLOCK. 'I will tolerate nothing less than complete obedience.'

SLAG turns and points at you. 'Why do we discuss our battle plans with a human child in our midst?' he demands. 'How do we know that our every move will not be observed and reported to our enemies, the Decepticons?'

*If you tell them you can help them in their mission, turn to page **41***
*If you leave them right now, turn to page **40***

'Don't mind me,' you say angrily. 'If you think I'm here to spy on you, I'll go!'

The Dinobots say nothing. Most of them are not sure whether to trust you, and the one called SLAG just sneers. Only the lumbering SLUDGE believes you can help them.

You march away from them into the swampy jungle. Pulling your way through thick vines and creepers, you soon come to a river. You happen to glance up and see a winged shape soaring through the mist towards you.

If you call out, turn to page 53
If you ignore it and carry on, turn to page 54

GRIMLOCK himself explains to you why they have gathered here. 'Somehow, two Decepticons called RAVAGE and LASERBEAK have come here out of the future. I suspect that they arrived with you – they have the power to disguise themselves as cassettes, so you may not even have noticed them.'

'What are they after?' you ask.

'Not far from here is the spot where our spaceship, the Ark, crash-landed on Earth. All the Transformers, both Autobots and Decepticons, lie asleep within and will not awaken for millions of years. We suspect that RAVAGE and LASERBEAK hope to find the Ark and destroy all the Autobots while they lie helpless!'

This talk of spaceships reminds you of the saucer you saw in Disneyland. Could it have anything to do with the Ark? You tell the Dinobots everything that happened to you.

Turn to page **58**

A shadow glides through the grey sky above you. 'Wait, SLUDGE, you lumbering brute!' shouts down a harsh robotic voice. You look up and see a metallic pterosaur descending through the mist.

'SWOOP,' says SLUDGE to the newcomer. 'What are you doing here?'

'Saving our leader's hide, for one thing,' replies SWOOP sourly as he lands on a stout tree branch. With his great wings folded he looks like a vulture. 'He ran into some trouble fighting a Decepticon — might've been the end of him if I hadn't dive-bombed in at the last moment!'

You realize that the fight he is describing must be the disturbance that you and SLUDGE were trying to get away from. You don't say anything about it, though. You like SLUDGE, and don't want SWOOP to think he is a coward.

At this moment, three more robot dinosaurs stomp into view. SLUDGE whispers to you that the tyrannosaurus who leads them is GRIMLOCK. The others are SLAG and SNARL.

Turn to page 38

SLUDGE yells to distract RAVAGE and then lumbers forward.

RAVAGE turns. Somehow, his metal jaws look evil. 'SLUDGE, you fool !' he hisses. 'You are a sitting target for my armour-piercing missiles.'

He is telling the truth. SLUDGE moves too slowly on the dry land. Before he can attack RAVAGE, the Decepticon shoots his missiles. There is a ruddy glow as their thrusters ignite. You notice that GRIMLOCK has got out of the mud and is heading towards RAVAGE. Your enemy is about to meet his end, but that is small consolation for you and SLUDGE. As the proton missiles streak towards you, you know that this is

THE END

SLUDGE lifts his foot and brings it down hard. A violent tremor shudders through the ground, unbalancing RAVAGE at the moment he fires his missile. The deadly proton missile shoots wide of the mark, it misses its intended target by several metres.

GRIMLOCK struggles out of the mud. 'Now, RAVAGE, we can resume our battle!' he roars.

RAVAGE glares at you and SLUDGE. With a wild snarl, he turns and runs off into the undergrowth. SLUDGE starts to lumber in pursuit, but GRIMLOCK calls him back. 'You cannot catch him now,' says the Dinobot leader. 'None can find RAVAGE when he does not wish to be found.'

At that moment there comes a harsh shriek from the sky. Looking up, you see a robot pterodactyl spiralling towards you.

Turn to page 34

Despite your fear, you manage to walk steadily towards the form amid the trees. As you draw near, you hear the slow, contented growl deep in its throat. It is almost like a purr. The great cat lies crouched, ready to uncurl in a single mighty bound towards you. Now you can see its green-gold eyes and the curve of its fangs. For an instant you share the intimacy of hunter and victim; and then, for you, it is

THE END

The thorny branches snag your clothes and scratch your skin painfully, but you manage to scramble up into a small tree. From your new perch, you peer down into the forest.

It is not long before your pursuer breaks cover and comes to slink around the base of your tree. It is a huge sabre-tooth tiger with wickedly sharp fangs and a hungry gleam in its eye. It is unable to climb the tree and, realizing that it has been outwitted, utters a sullen growl and then slopes off.

You give it twenty minutes or so to get well away from here before jumping down from the tree to continue on your way.

Turn to page 52

You crash through a thicket and race away from the creature that is stalking you. Swarms of gnats cloud around you, and the sweat pouring from your brow soon blinds you, but still you stumble on. In the end you come to a clearing amid the trees, and here you stop.

Lying on top of a low boulder is a large robot cat. At least, it looks something like a cat, though it has two gleaming silver missiles attached to its steel-grey flanks.

You take a step back, almost too startled to be frightened. Is this the feline creature you were running from? If so, how did it get ahead of you?

'I am RAVAGE,' it murmurs lazily, slipping down from the boulder in no particular hurry. 'And you, human, are my prey —'

If you surrender to RAVAGE, turn to page 51
If you try to escape, turn to page 50

'How can you hope to flee from me?' snarls RAVAGE as you turn to run. 'I am the master of stealth and hunting!'

You hear the foliage behind you part with barely a whisper as the crafty Decepticon prowls in pursuit of you. You stagger on, but you feel tired enough to drop.

A creature rises from the bushes nearby and slinks out to block your path. But it is not RAVAGE — it is a sabre-tooth tiger. It is far larger than any tiger of modern times, and its gleaming white canines are some 25 cm long!

You hear RAVAGE behind you. The sabre-tooth notices him also — but does not realize he is a robot. It assumes he is another tiger poaching on its territory. With a terrifying roar it leaps right over your head and lands on RAVAGE's back. You know that for all its strength, the sabre-tooth will not survive for more than a minute against RAVAGE. While they thrash about in mortal combat, you make good your escape.

Turn to page 52

'The fight between humans and Decepticons is a battle to the death,' replies RAVAGE, responding to your surrender with a cold chuckle. 'There can be no prisoners of war.'

He opens his razor-sharp jaws and lopes towards you. You know suddenly that this is

THE END

A familiar voice calls to you. You are relieved to discover that the Dinobot SLUDGE has come back to look for you. He bobs his massive head down in front of yours.

'I've changed my mind,' you say. 'This jungle is turning out to be more dangerous than I'd expected!'

'Let me give you a ride,' says SLUDGE. 'Climb up on to my neck and we'll rejoin GRIMLOCK.'

Turn to page 33

You assume that the winged shape is SWOOP. So the Dinobots changed their minds about trusting you. You yell his name up into the mist.

The voice that replies is cold with evil. 'A fatal mistake, young human,' it hisses gleefully. 'I am LASERBEAK, one of the Decepticons . . . '

With a screech of igniting jets, LASERBEAK sweeps in to the attack. He looks like a monstrous phantom emerging from the fog, with twin ruby lasers glowing along his hooked beak.

Suddenly another, larger, winged figure appears. This time it really is SWOOP − and in the nick of time! LASERBEAK screams in rage and spins to one side to avoid SWOOP's attack. Rather than counter-attacking with his lasers, the Decepticon speeds away across the marsh.

'I must apologise,' says SWOOP as he alights beside you. 'I can see now that you are no friend of the Decepticons − let us go back to join the other Dinobots.'

Turn to page 41

You assume it is just SWOOP. Well, if he has come to apologise to you then you are not interested! You storm off through the forest. As a damp twig breaks under your foot, there is a triumphant laugh from the winged figure above.

'Hold still, little human,' it hisses as it drops through the curtain of fog. 'In another moment I'll have you in my laser sights.'

It is not SWOOP at all — it's one of the Evil Decepticons! If you cannot get away then he will burn you to a crisp with his searing ruby lasers.

Will you try to hide? If so, turn to page 55
If you shout for help, turn to page 56

You hide behind the trunk of a tree, but the flying Decepticon screeches towards you. You see the gleam of his lasers as they are energized — like the eyes of a hellhound. There is a burst of scarlet light, an instant of agony, and then

THE END

You yell at the top of your lungs as you sprint from the flying Decepticon. You have no idea whether the Dinobots are still nearby. And would they bother to help you anyway?

'There is no one here to help you,' jeers the Decepticon as he streaks through the air towards you. 'All your shouts are doing is making things easy for me. There – now I have you square in my laser sights!'

You throw yourself down into the mud just as two fine ruby beams sizzle overhead and char the bark on a nearby tree. There is a shriek from the hovering Decepticon. 'Bah, human! You will die anyway – why bother to delay it?'

You lie helpless in the mud. You know his next shot will destroy you.

A metal head swings like a battering ram through the trees and slams into the Decepticon. He is thrown through the air, but manages to stay aloft. Seeing SLUDGE – again in brontosaur form – beside you, he hisses in rage and soars up into the sky.

'Ouch,' says SLUDGE. 'Butting LASERBEAK like that has given me a headache. I guess I should leave that kind of thing to SLAG!'

You are pleased he came along when he did. It seems that the Dinobots have decided to trust you after all, so you go back with SLUDGE to rejoin them.

Turn to page 41

'I have been in this area for several days,' says SWOOP. 'It is nothing to do with the Ark — that crash-landed on Earth centuries ago — but I did see a flying saucer landing in the hills to the east.'

GRIMLOCK is angry. 'Why didn't you report this earlier?'

'As I said, it has nothing to do with the Ark,' SWOOP replies.

'Still, we must investigate. Wherever this saucer comes from, its owners have the power to travel in time. It was their device, unearthed after millions of years, that brought our young friend here. Come!'

Rapidly transforming to their saurian forms, the Dinobots hurry after their leader. After an hour or so you begin to reach higher ground. The ground is drier and sunlight pierces through the mist. SNARL grows stronger as his solar panels draw energy from the light.

Suddenly a real dinosaur — a triceratops — stomps from the undergrowth right in front of you! You give a yelp and scramble back towards the Dinobots.

'Hey, a triceratops,' says SLUDGE. 'It's a dead ringer for you, SLAG.'

'*Dead* is what it'll be, all right,' replies SLAG. A sheet of white-hot flame shoots out from his mouth. You expect to hear the triceratops roar in pain as it is engulfed, but the flame doesn't seem to bother it.

'Real dinosaurs became extinct millions of years ago!' calls out SWOOP. Chortling, he flies through the triceratops as though it weren't there. You notice a cine-projector hidden in the bushes. As you pass in front of it, the triceratops disappears.

'It's just a hologram — an illusion,' grunts SNARL. 'Somebody's trying to scare off unwelcome visitors.' He walks right through the holographic image. You reach out and turn the projector off.

'See,' calls out SWOOP from above, 'the flying saucer came down in that cave there!'

You survey the cave entrance. It is too low for the huge Dinobots to enter – if you go in, you must go alone!

If you offer to enter the cave on your own, turn to page
60
If you refuse to go in, turn to page **62**

'Very brave!' says GRIMLOCK approvingly. Even SLAG nods in respect.

You slip into the shadows inside the cave and find a shelf of rock which you crawl along. Looking back, you see the Dinobots clustered around the cave entrance. SLUDGE waves to you.

You soon reach the end of the rock shelf. You find yourself looking out over a large underground cavern. The saucer which you saw in Disneyland rests on the floor of the cavern. When you saw it before (later?) it was coated with centuries of dust, but here it sparkles like new.

In front of the saucer, two thin aliens are setting up some kind of scientific equipment. You can also see another projector. Now you understand who was trying to scare you off. They have small round bodies, and several eyes all around their heads. They are talking to each other in a weird, high-pitched language.

Something makes you glance up. On a ledge just above you, you see the Decepticon known as RAVAGE. He looks like a huge black panther waiting to pounce. He is so intent on watching the aliens that he hasn't noticed you.

Will you shout a warning to the aliens? If so, turn to page 64
If you try to creep down to the saucer, turn to page 67

'You coward!' jeers SLAG. 'I have no patience with weaklings.' He strides off down the hill. The other Dinobots murmur and watch you from the corner of their eyes.

Only SLUDGE is sympathetic. 'Nobody can blame you for being afraid,' he says. 'I'm armour-plated and weigh fifty tonnes, but I'm not all that sure I'd want to go into the cave alone!'

The others accept that you are not a warrior. Only SWOOP is unmoved by SLUDGE's words. 'That's because you're a coward, too, SLUDGE,' he says as he takes to the air.

Turn to page 63

With no way to get back to your own time, you have no choice but to live out your days with the Dinobots. SLUDGE does his best to make you forget the future, and you share a lifetime of fabulous adventures with him. But you cannot help thinking of your family and friends. Looking up at the stars one night, you realize that you will grow old and die millions of years before they are born. You cannot help feeling alone and sad.

THE END

Your voice echoes from the cavern walls. The aliens start to chatter excitedly and wave their spindly arms. They do not understand what you are trying to tell them. They are more curious than frightened.

What you *have* succeeded in doing is drawing RAVAGE's attention. His eyes glitter with savage hatred as he bounds down from his ledge. He lands on top of you, knocking all the breath out of your body. You think it is the end, but he merely glares into your eyes for an instant and then leaps down towards the aliens. You will never know why he spared your life.

The other Decepticon, LASERBEAK has also emerged from the shadows. He swoops down and kills one of the aliens with a burst of photonic energy. The other alien sees RAVAGE rushing towards him and starts to run. RAVAGE reaches him at the saucer's door. The force of his leap carries them both inside.

Turn to page 65

You can hear the Dinobots calling to you and you wave, assuring them that you are unhurt. 'Where are RAVAGE and LASERBEAK?' demands GRIMLOCK.

You nervously approach the saucer. LASERBEAK swept inside just behind RAVAGE, but there is no sign of either of them now. The saucer is empty. You assume that the alien managed to flee into the past or future, but it seems that he accidentally took the Decepticons with him!

You look around the saucer carefully. You are hoping to find one of the metal spheres which could return you to your own time, but the search is fruitless. The only device you can find is a bulky rifle. Are you stranded in the past forever, then?

*If you wish to use the rifle, turn to page **68***
*If you go back to where the Dinobots are waiting, turn to page **63***

You clamber over the edge of the rock shelf and quietly make your way down to the floor of the cavern. Moving on tiptoe, you approach the open door of the saucer. The two aliens are hard at work taking readings from their instruments, and do not see you. You glance up into the shadows. Even though you know where RAVAGE is hiding, it is very difficult to see him in the dim light.

You reach the saucer and dart inside, still unnoticed. It does not take you long to find the metal sphere that brought you back in time. You have only to turn the dial on the side and you would be returned to your own time. You are about to do it, but then a thought crosses your mind. If you leave RAVAGE and LASERBEAK here, they may outwit the Dinobots and succeed in reaching the Ark. You cannot allow that!

Running to the door, you start yelling: 'Come on, Decepticons! Come and get me!'

The two little aliens look up in surprise and begin to jabber at you. Then they see RAVAGE and LASER-BEAK rushing furiously towards you, and pass out in a dead faint.

'Prepare to die, human,' snarls RAVAGE as he reaches you.

'Not just yet,' you reply, twisting the dial on the time-sphere . . .

Turn to page **69**

67

The device is a Stasis Gun, with the power to 'freeze' objects in time. Objects – or *people*. In sudden excitement, you realize it is your one chance of getting back to your own time.

You turn to rifle until you are looking straight down into the nozzle. You find a button on the side and your finger touches it lightly. Although you are afraid, you seem to have no other choice. You press the button.

*Turn to page **70***

. . . You are ready for the time-travel on this occasion. Although it makes you giddy, you do not pass out. You see LASERBEAK and RAVAGE moving through a swirl of colour all around you. It is as though the three of you are being swept along in a rainbow-coloured whirl-wind.

At last the lights fade and you rematerialize in The Wizard's Cave in Disneyland. There is no sign of the two Decepticons now — either they slipped away very quickly or else they have got lost forever in the space-time continuum.

A scientist steps forward and takes the time-sphere out of your hand. 'You shouldn't play with that, kid,' he snaps. 'Who knows what it might do?'

You smile at him sheepishly. *He* may not know — but you do!

Turn to page 71

– The next thing you know, you are standing in the middle of a circle of scientist. cameramen, reporters and astonished onlookers. With a sigh of relief, you recognize the Wizard's Cave attraction in Disneyland!

'That's right, ladies and gentlemen,' a newsman is saying into his microphone. 'The figure that scientists found today in Disneyland, and have just brought out of suspended animation, seems to be – not the alien or caveman we'd expected – but a normal modern-day youngster!'

Turn to page 71

You have managed to return to the present day — but you have a lot of explaining to do.

Will anyone believe your story? Do you believe it yourself?

THE END

THE TRANSFORMERS™
PERIL FROM THE STARS
by Dave Morris

Evil Robots walk among us!

Earth has been invaded by the powerful robots from the distant planet Cybertron – the Heroic Autobots and their enemies, the Evil Decepticons. They can disguise their robot shapes as earthly machines and transform for battle at lightning speed. The battle between Good and Evil rages on Earth . . .

You are the hero of this book – suddenly you are thrust into the deadly struggle

You will meet the valiant Autobot JAZZ and help him fight against the evil STARSCREAM. But be careful – your actions will decide whether the Decepticon is defeated or whether he gets the terrible weapons he needs to overthrow the world!

If you collect Transformers™, this book is for you!

SBN 0 552 523151

T.R. BEAR: ENTER T.R.
by Terrance Dicks

It all started when Jimmy got a parcel from his Uncle Colin in America. The teddy bear inside was unlike any bear Jimmy had ever seen. He looked tough, and he was wearing glasses! According to the label, his name was Theodore Roosevelt, T.R. for short.

Jimmy soon found out that life with T.R. Bear was quite eventful . . .

SBN 0 552 523011

If you would like to receive a newsletter telling you about our new children's books, fill in the coupon with your name and address and send it to:

The Children's Books Editor,
Transworld Publishers Ltd.,
61–63 Uxbridge Road, Ealing,
London, W5 5SA

Name ..WAYNE Tuckfield..........

Address ..III MAXEY Rd...............

............Dagenham.................

...............essex....................

CHILDREN'S NEWSLETTER

LOUISE WREN

The Little Red Patient

The true story of Maddie, a disabled fox cub who
learned to live with humans